I0482503

# BEACH PARTY
## 24 PAGE COLORING BOOK

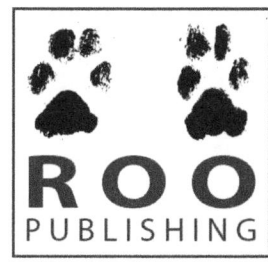

ROO
PUBLISHING

*Illustrations by Dani Kates*

Dear Colorer,

My name is Dani and I drew the pictures in this coloring book!
I'm an artist, a designer, and a HUGE fan of coloring.
When I buy a coloring book, the first thing I do is take a thin black pen and
draw tiny detailed lines and patterns to make the pictures more fun to color.
I love doing it so much that I decided to design my own coloring books with the
same type of detailed lines and fun patterns.

All of those details and lines make this is an adult style coloring book
but the pictures are a lot more fun to color!

This one is all about the beach.
Flip Flops, Beach bags, ice cream...and so much more!

So have fun, color something amazing and share it with me on social media!

**@DaniKatesColoringBooks**
**#DaniKatesColoringBooks**

XOXO,
Dani Kates

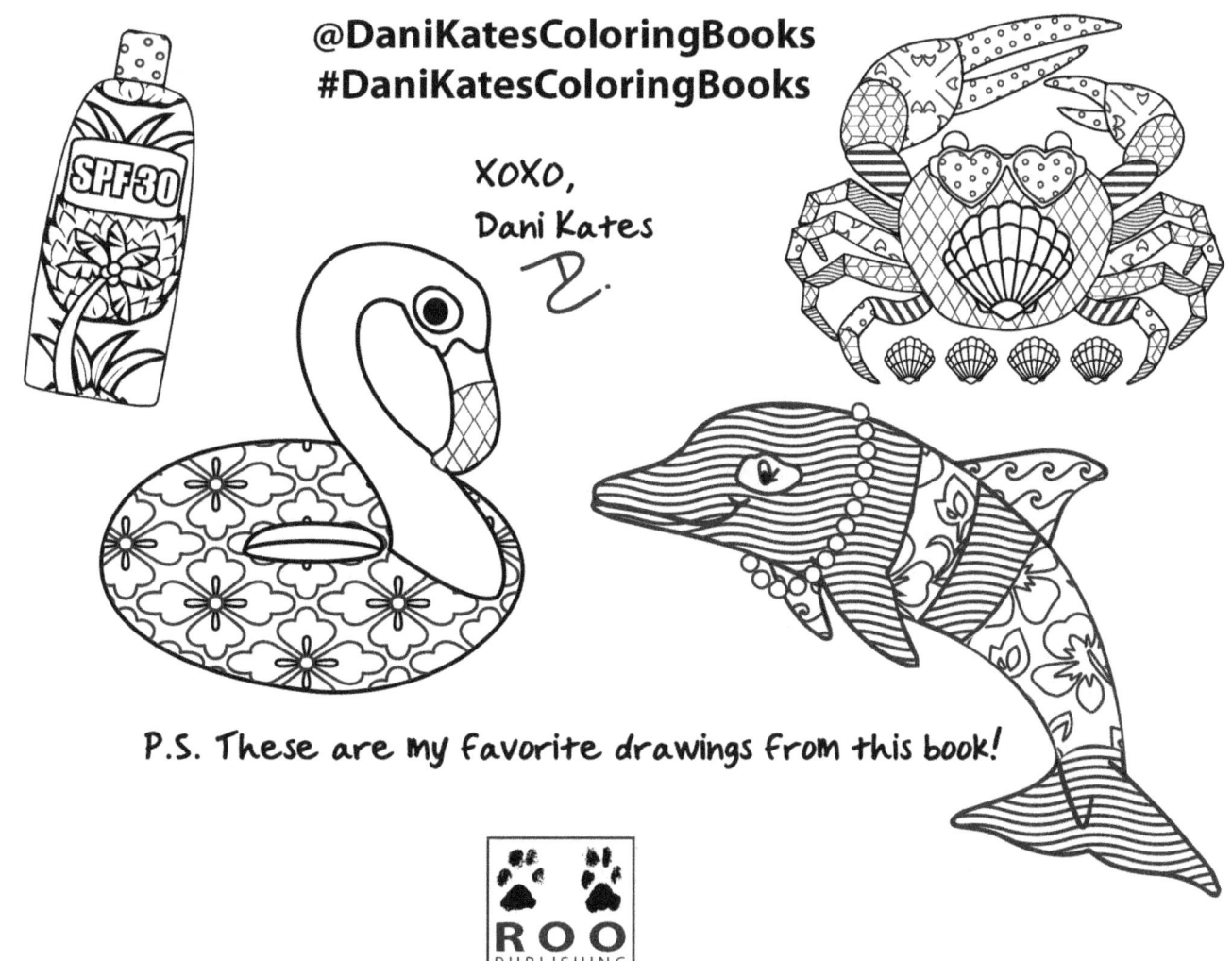

P.S. These are my favorite drawings from this book!

ROO
PUBLISHING

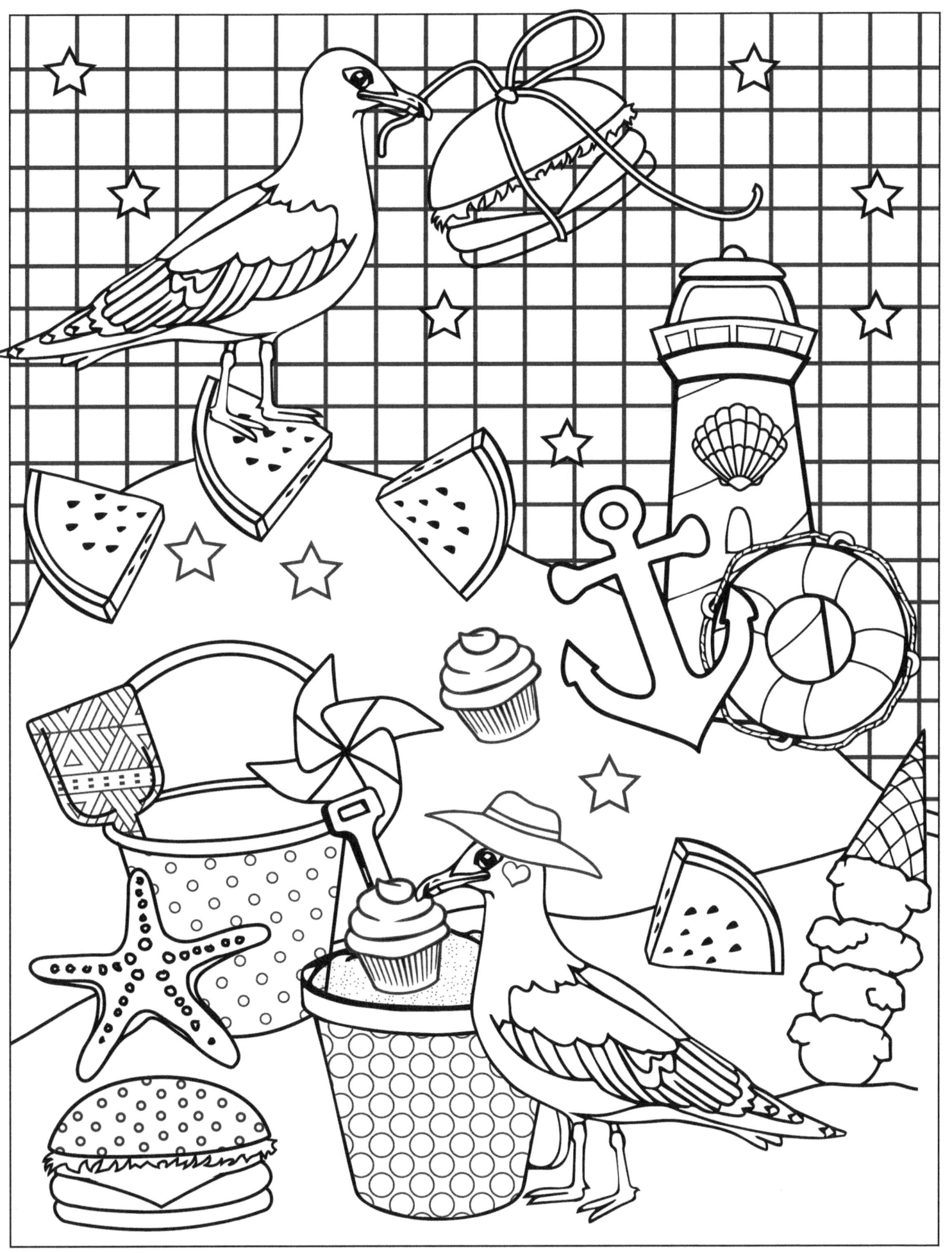

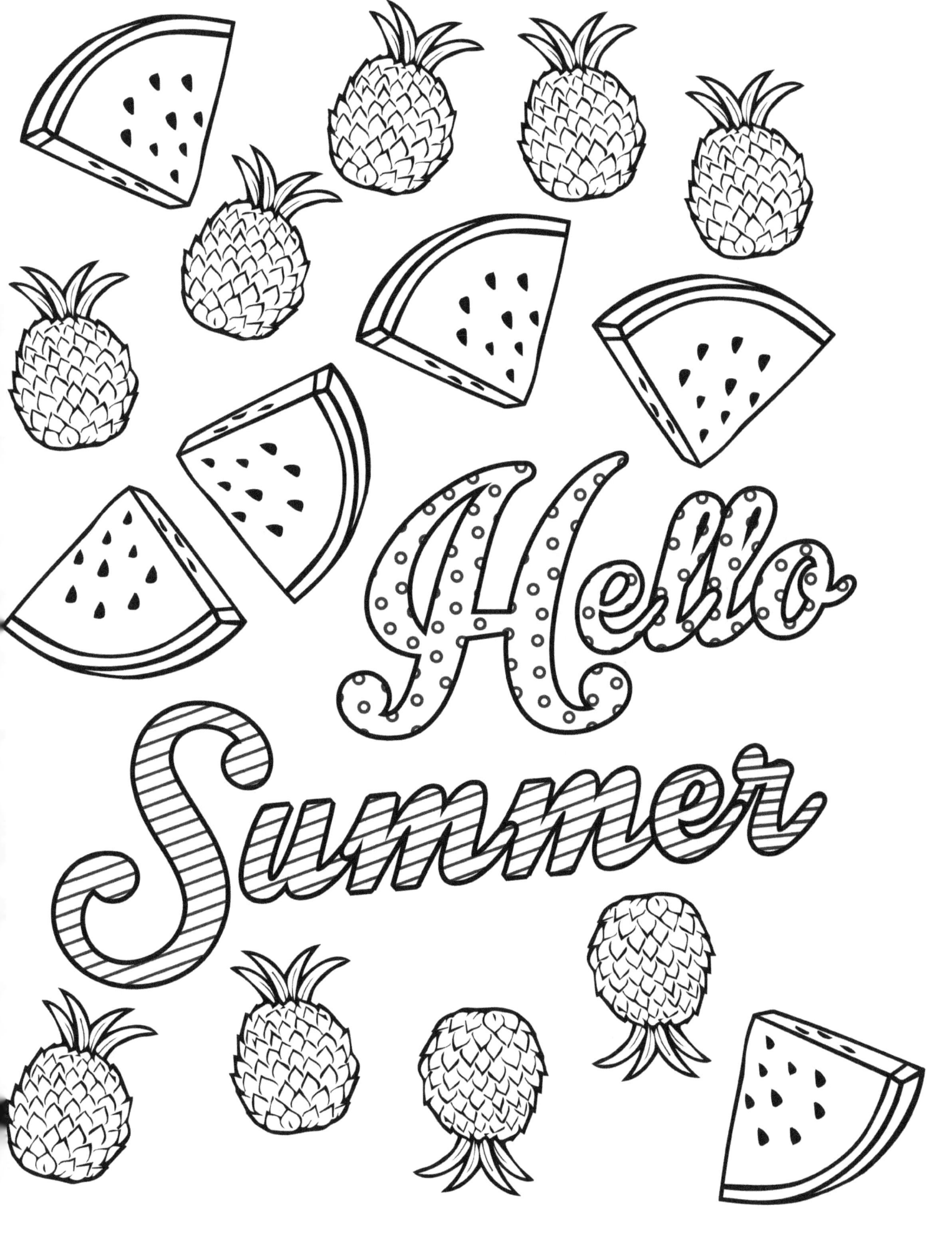

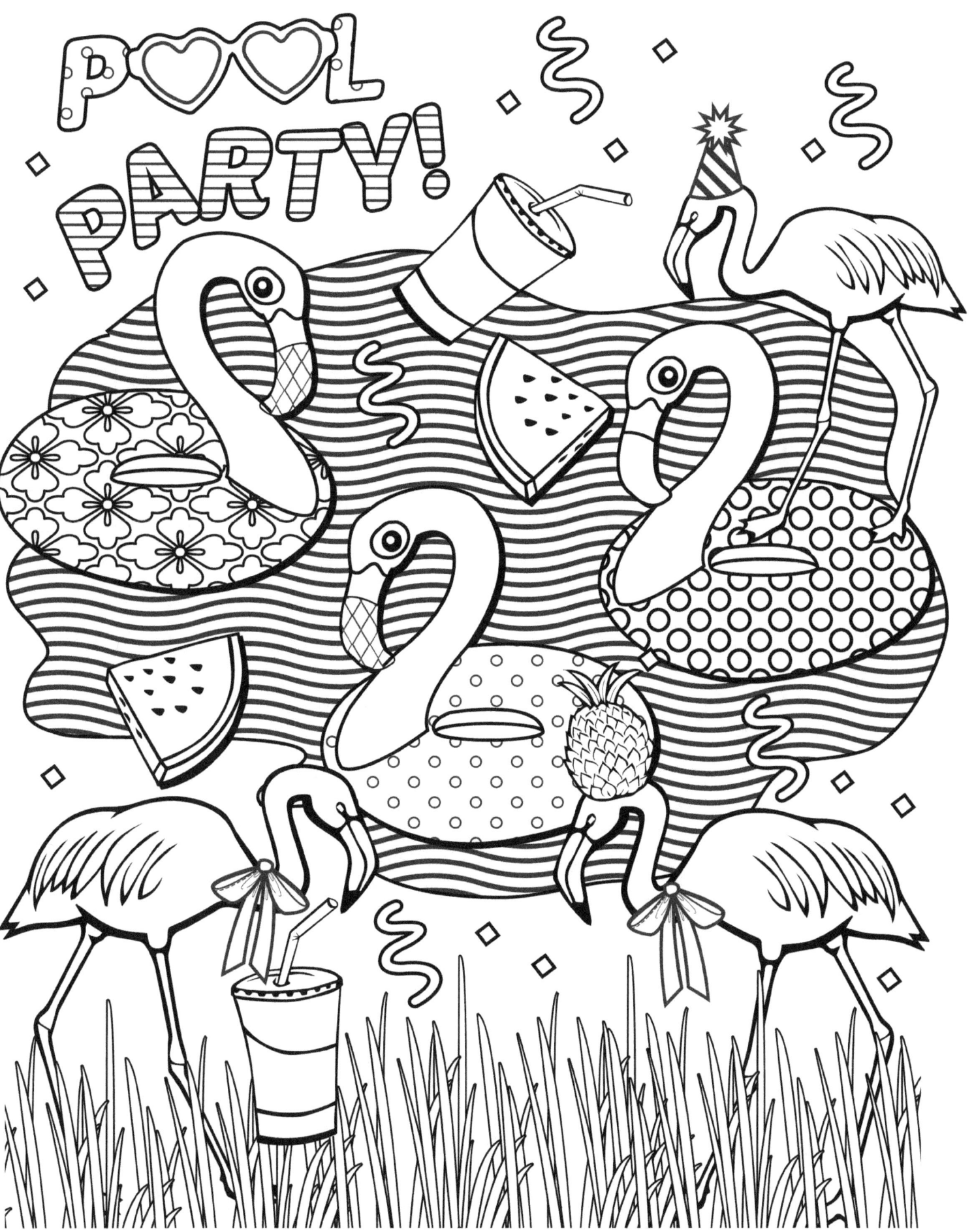

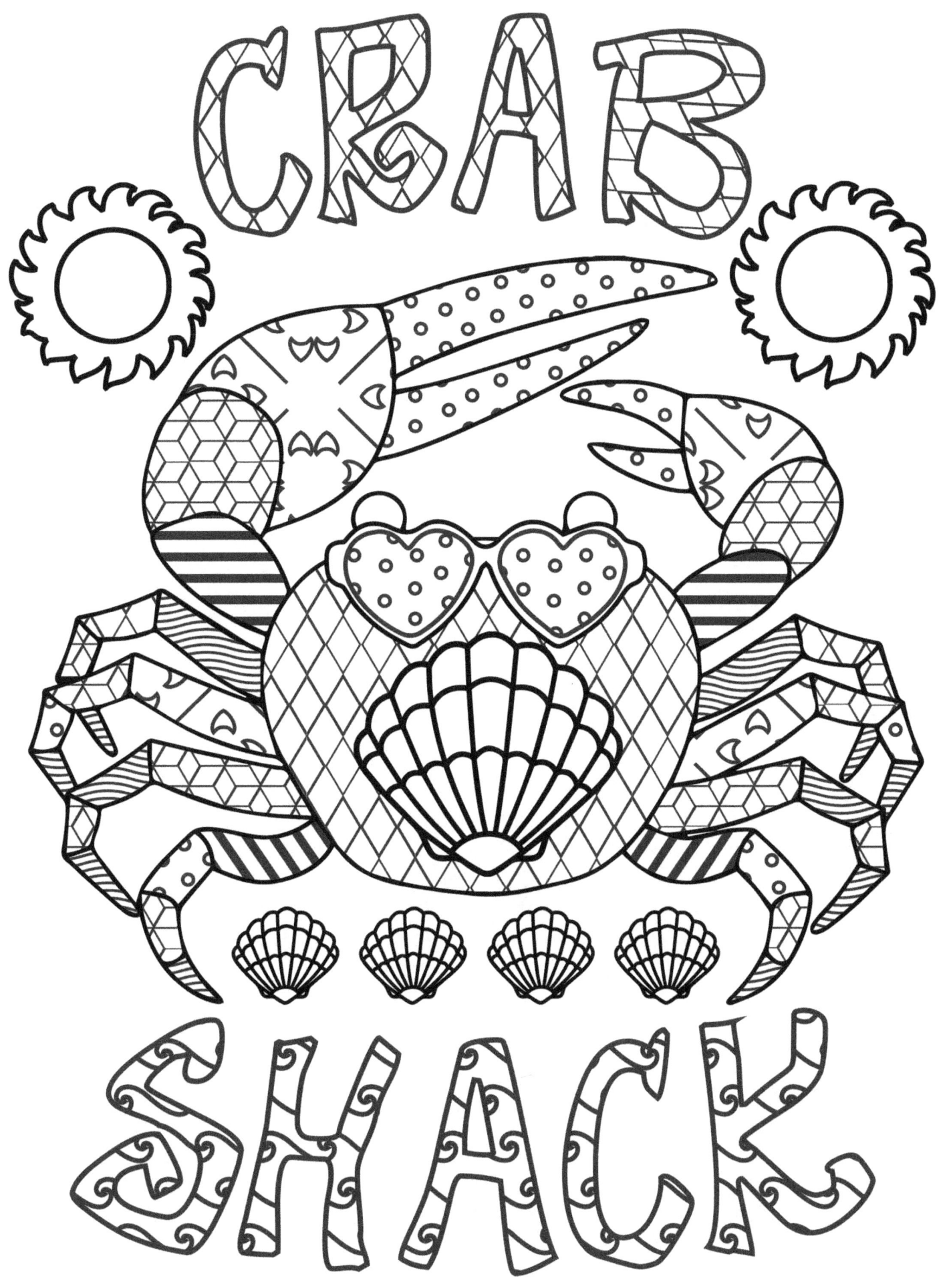

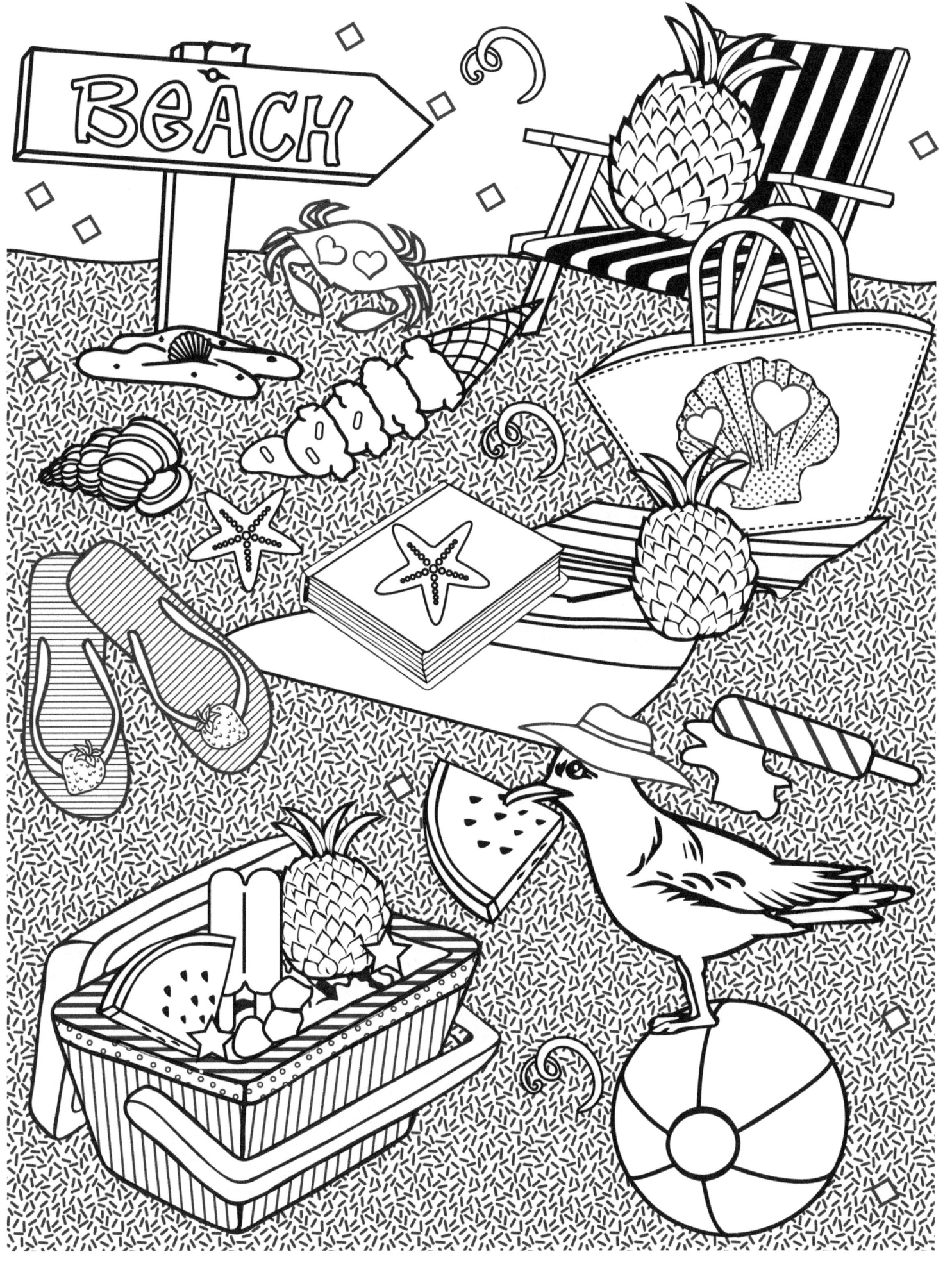

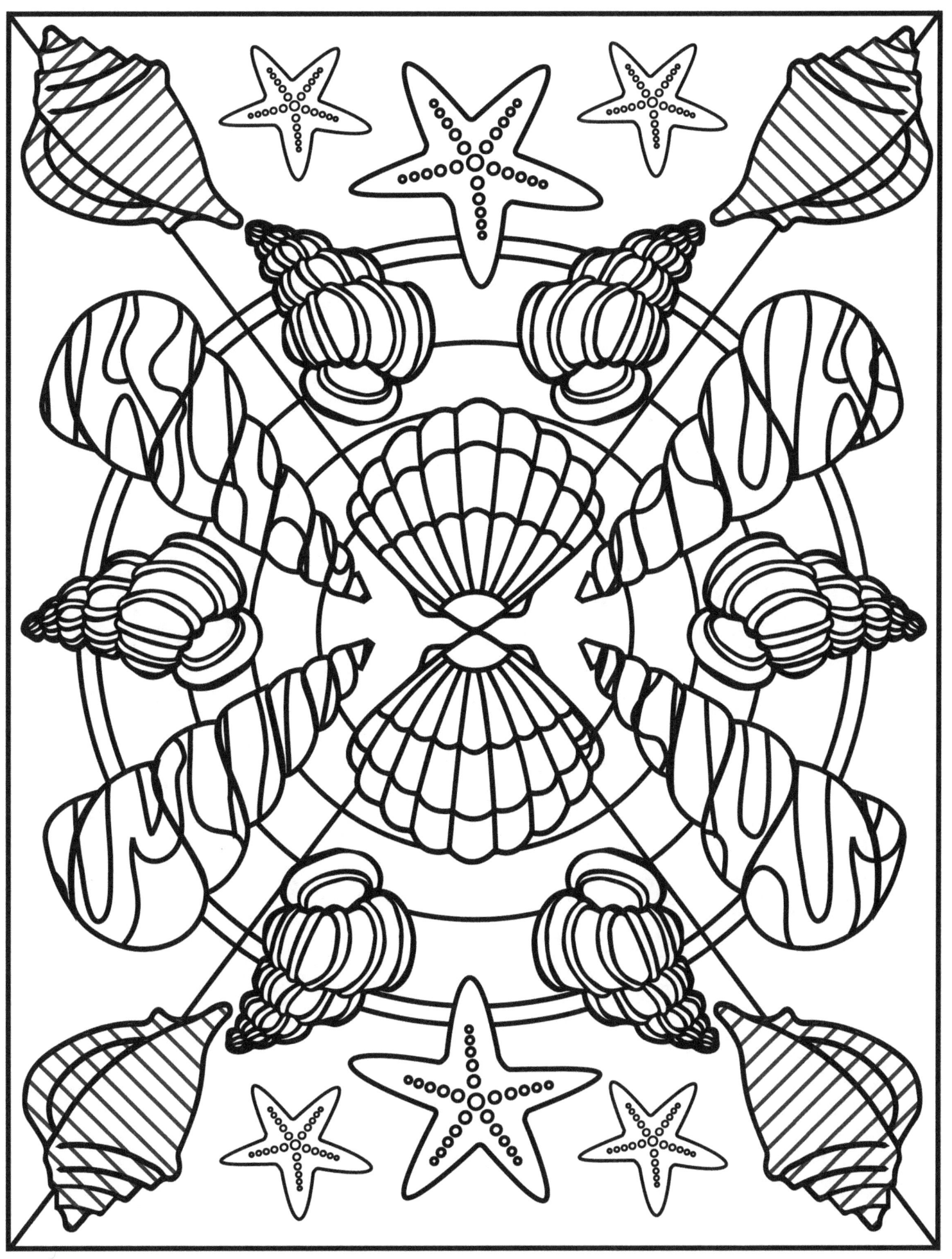

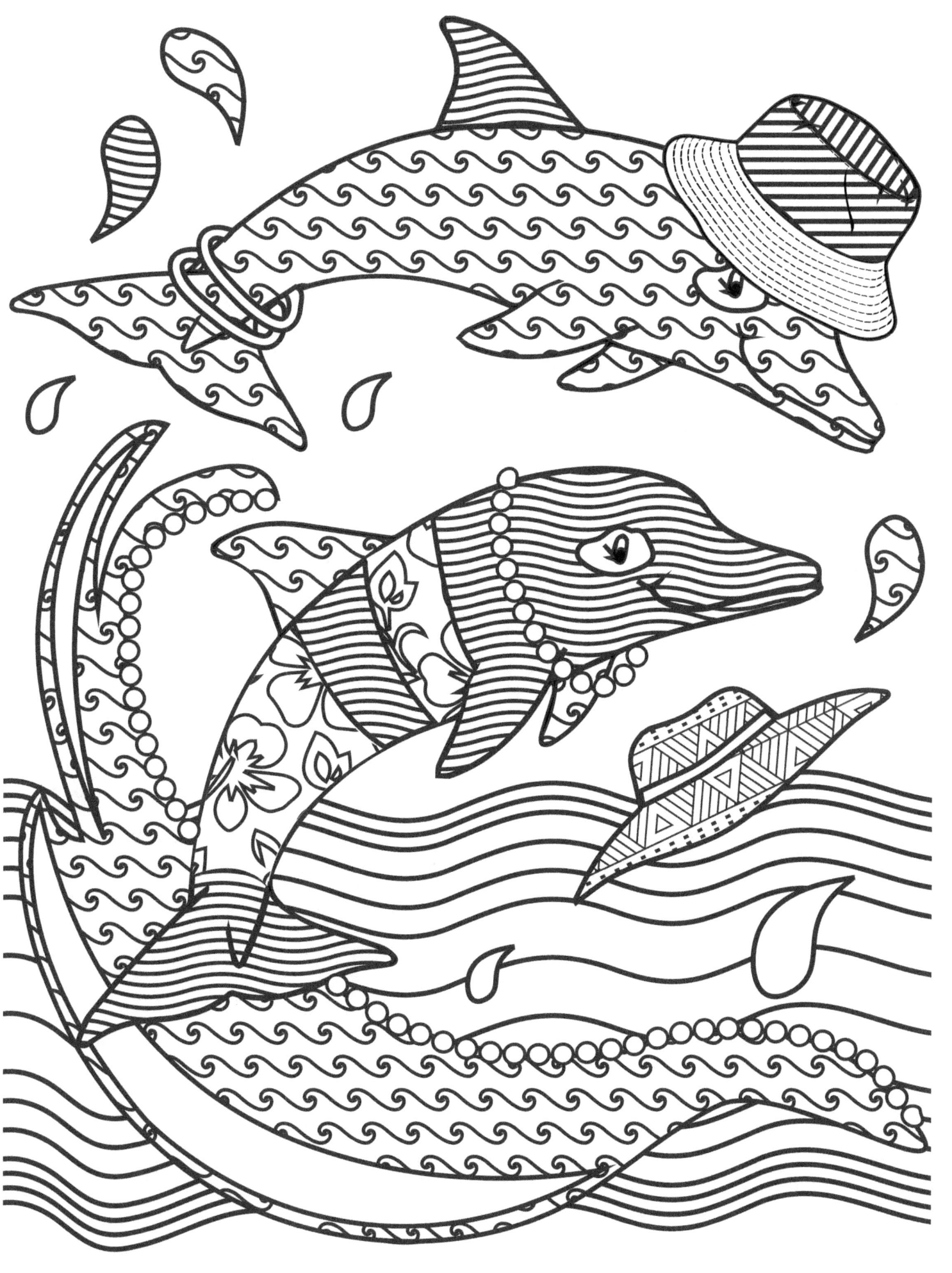

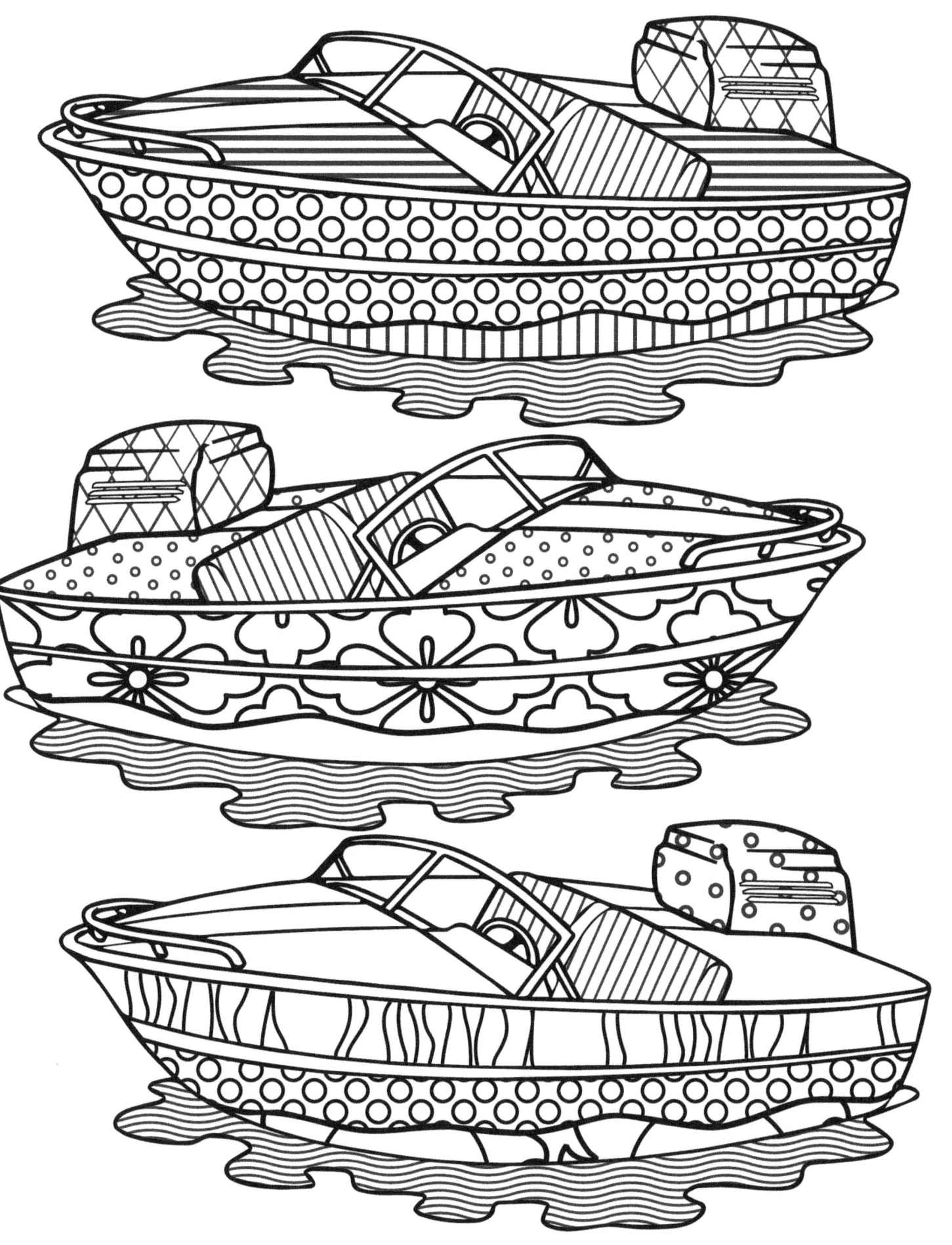

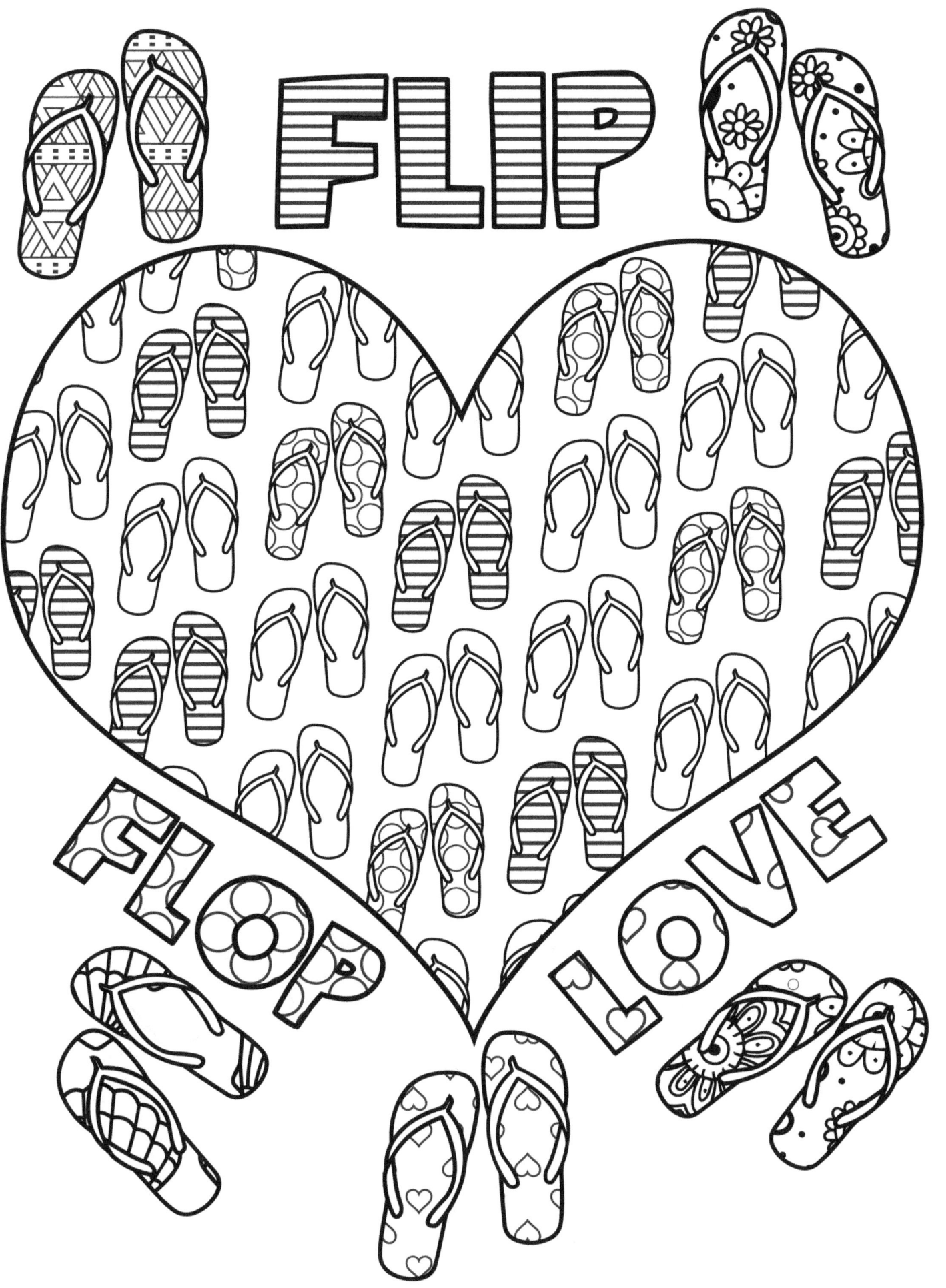

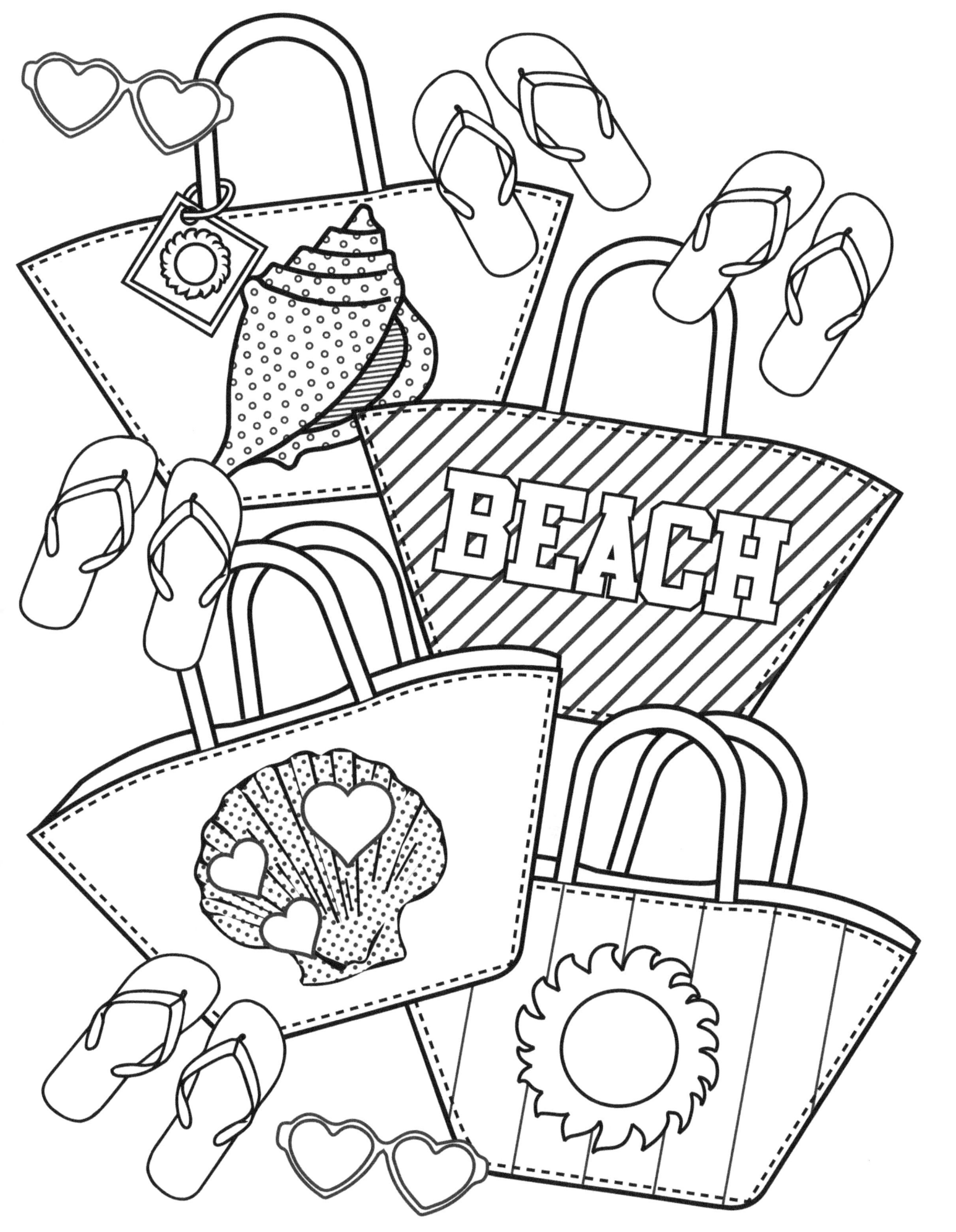

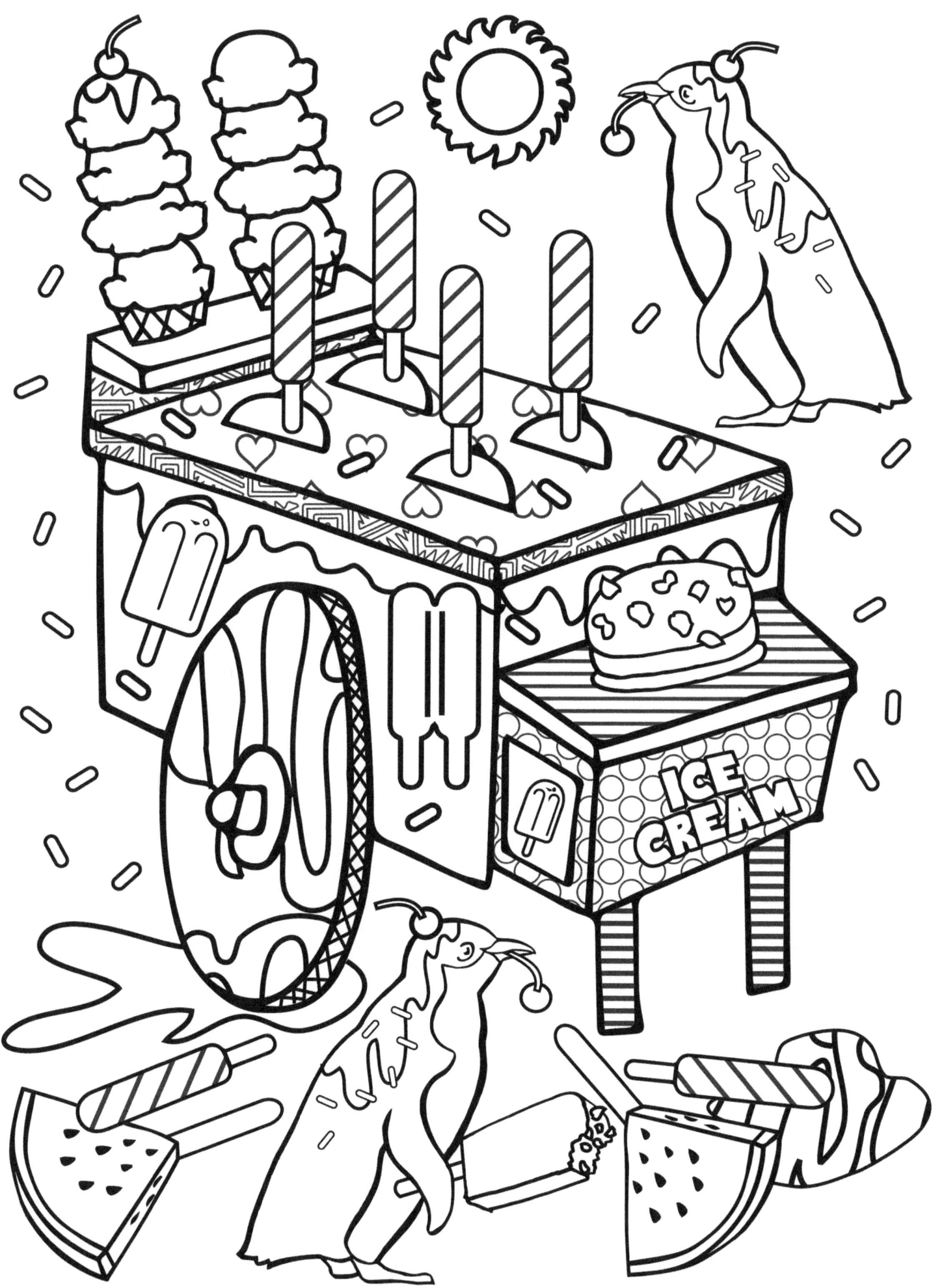

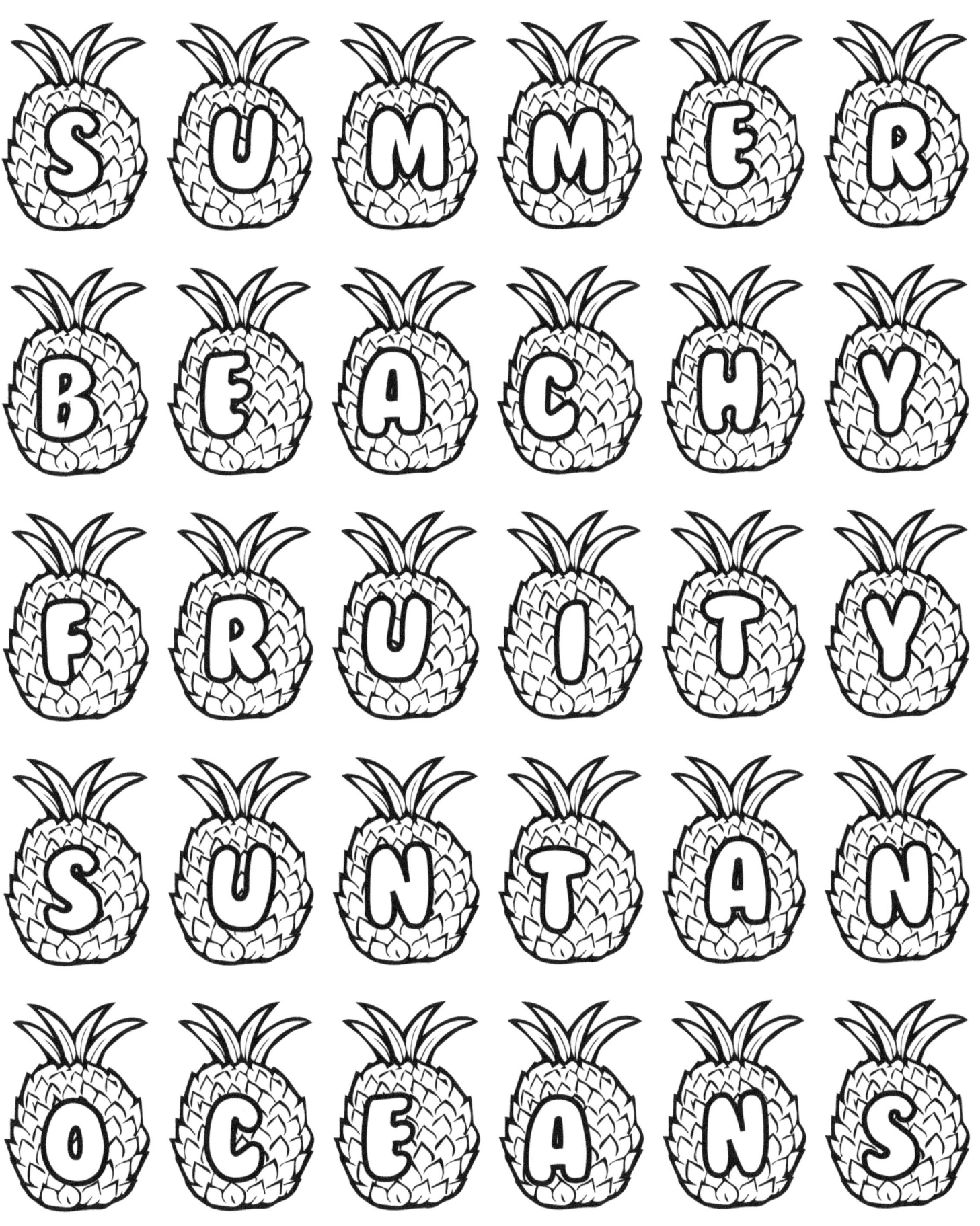

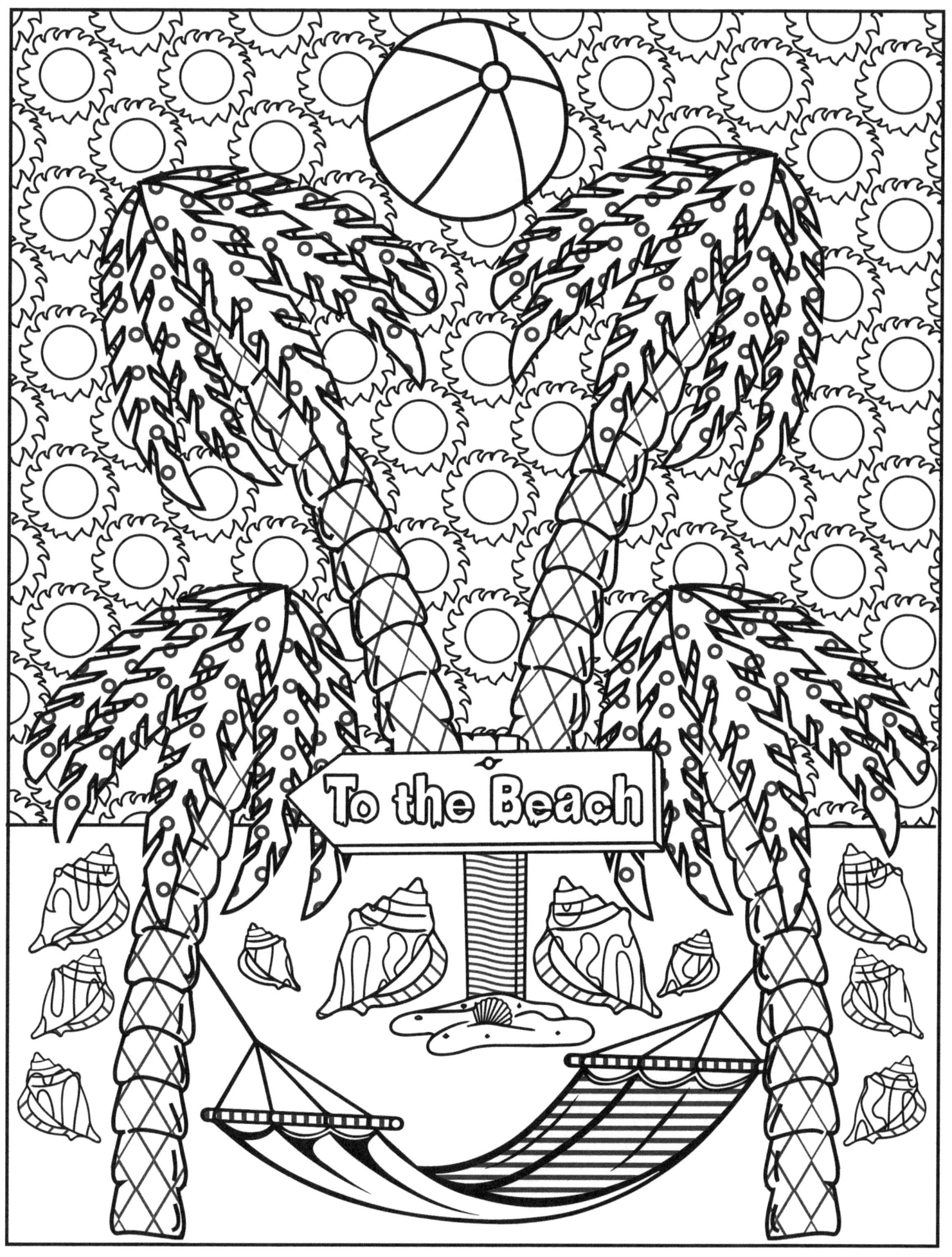

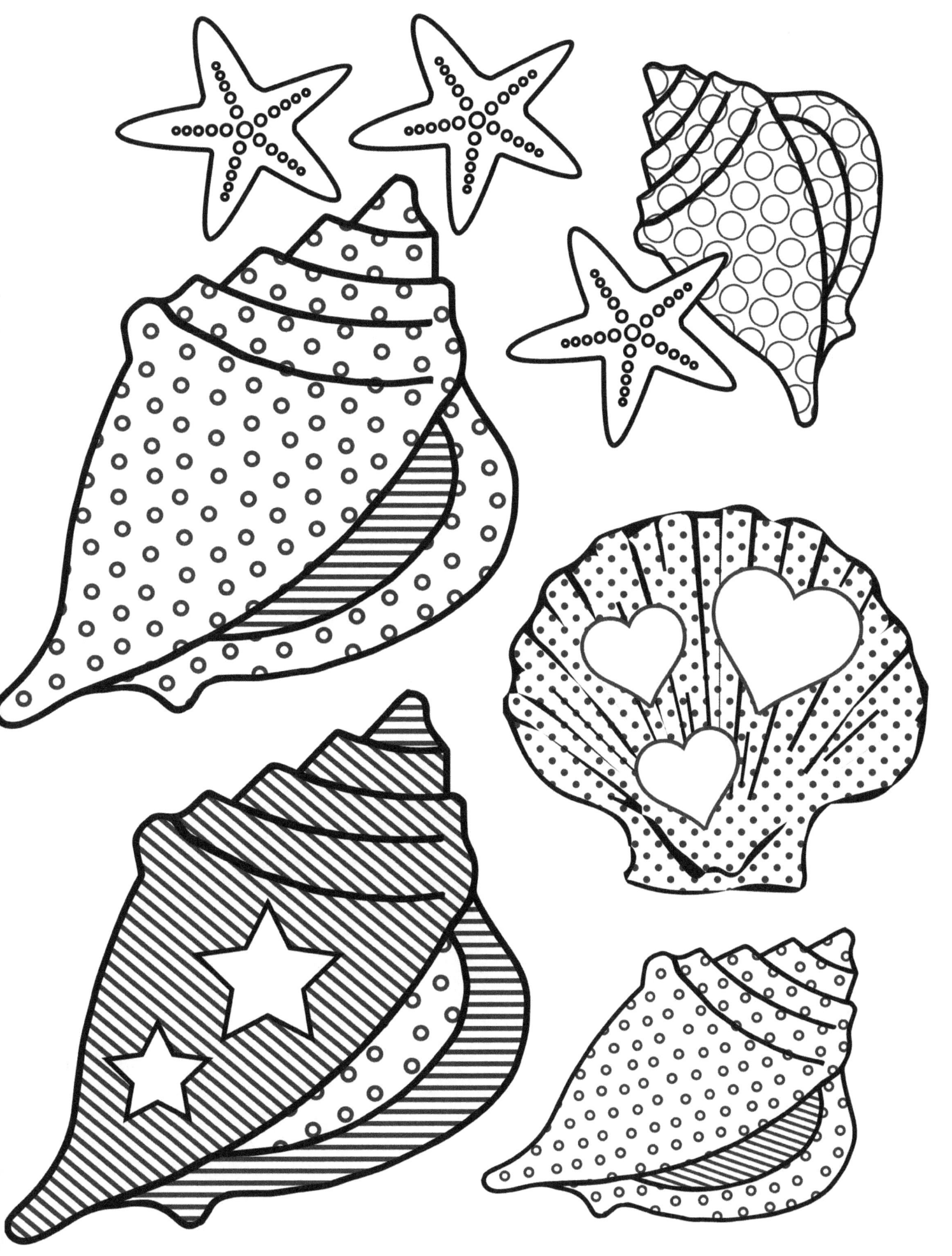

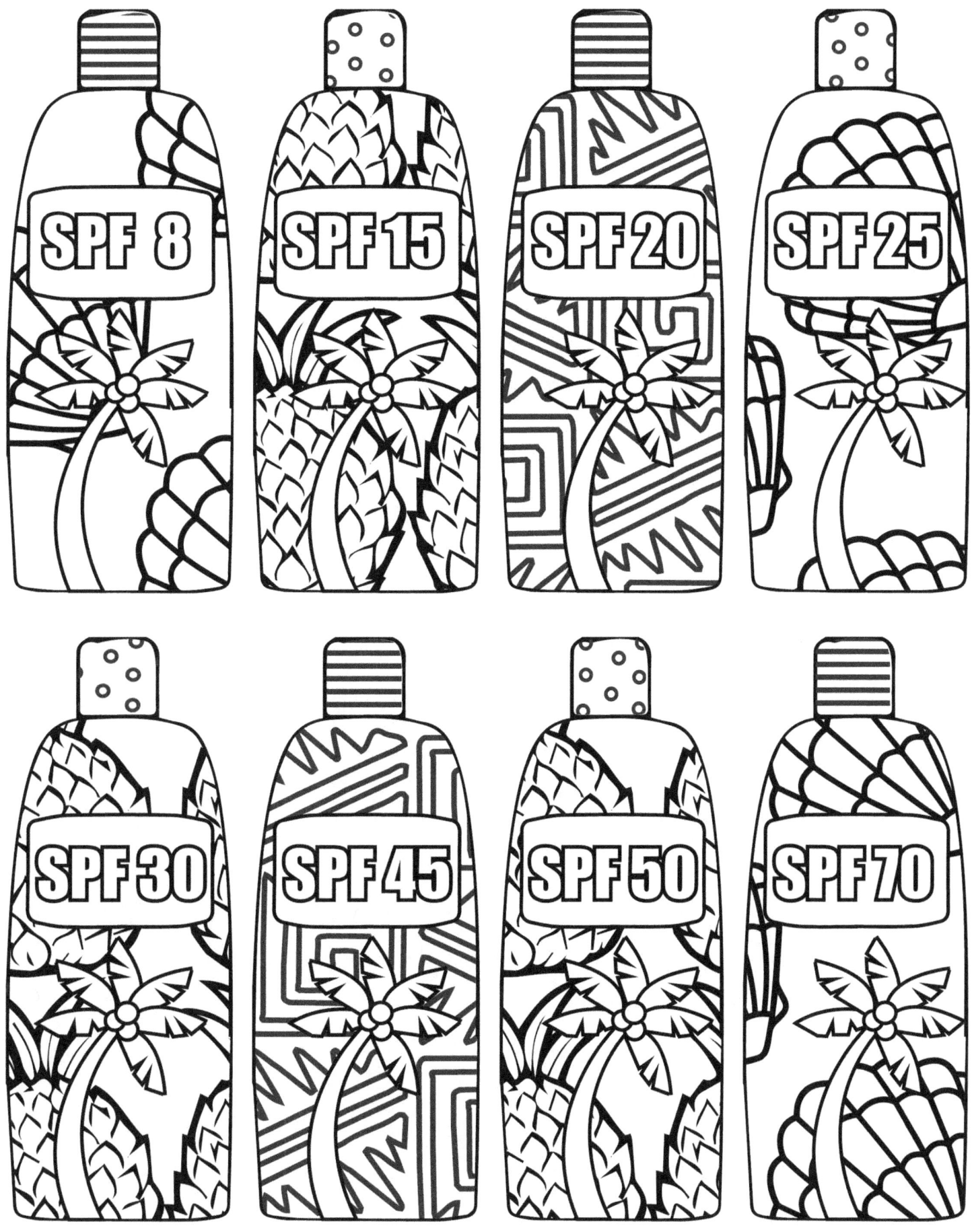

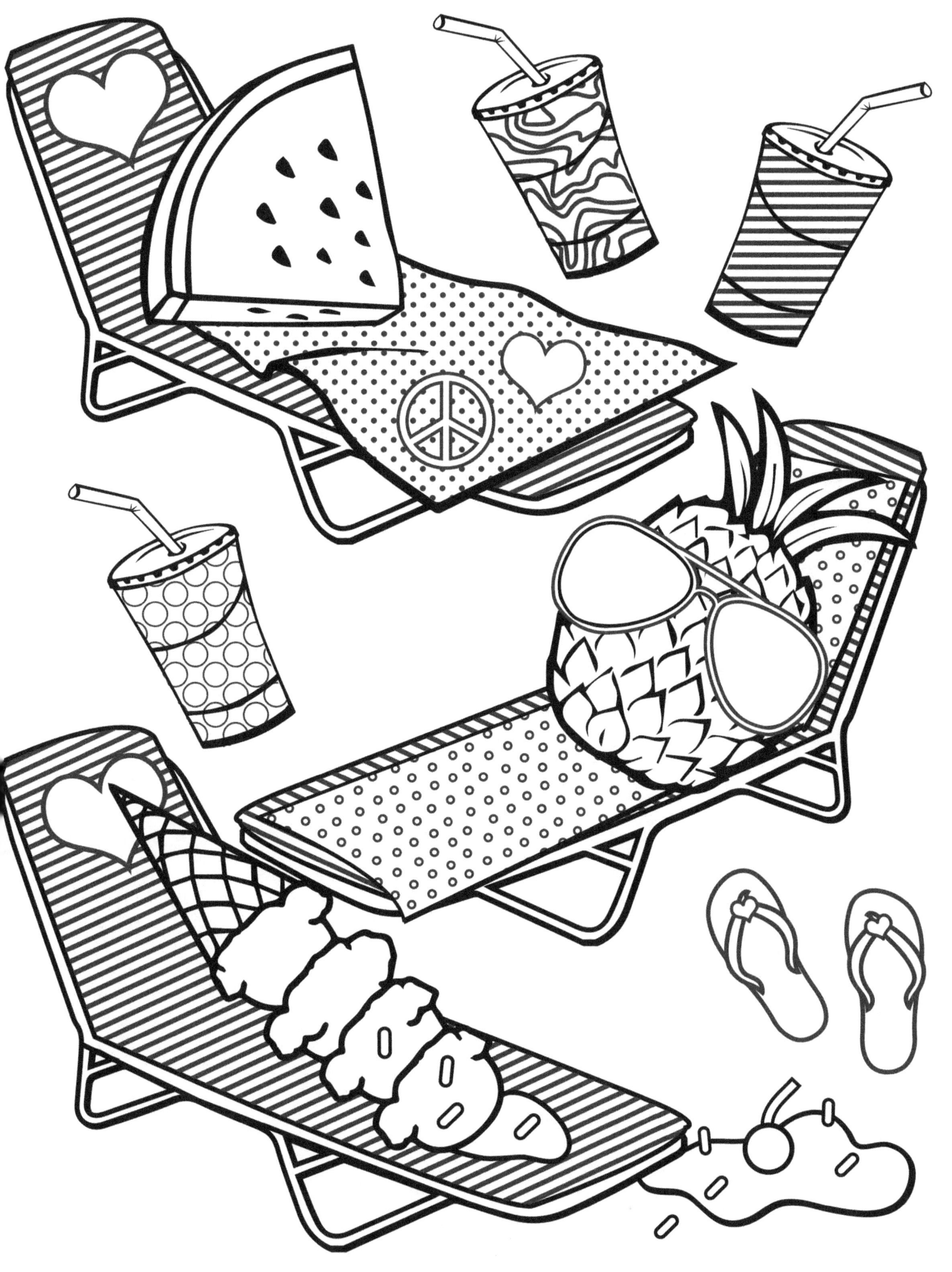

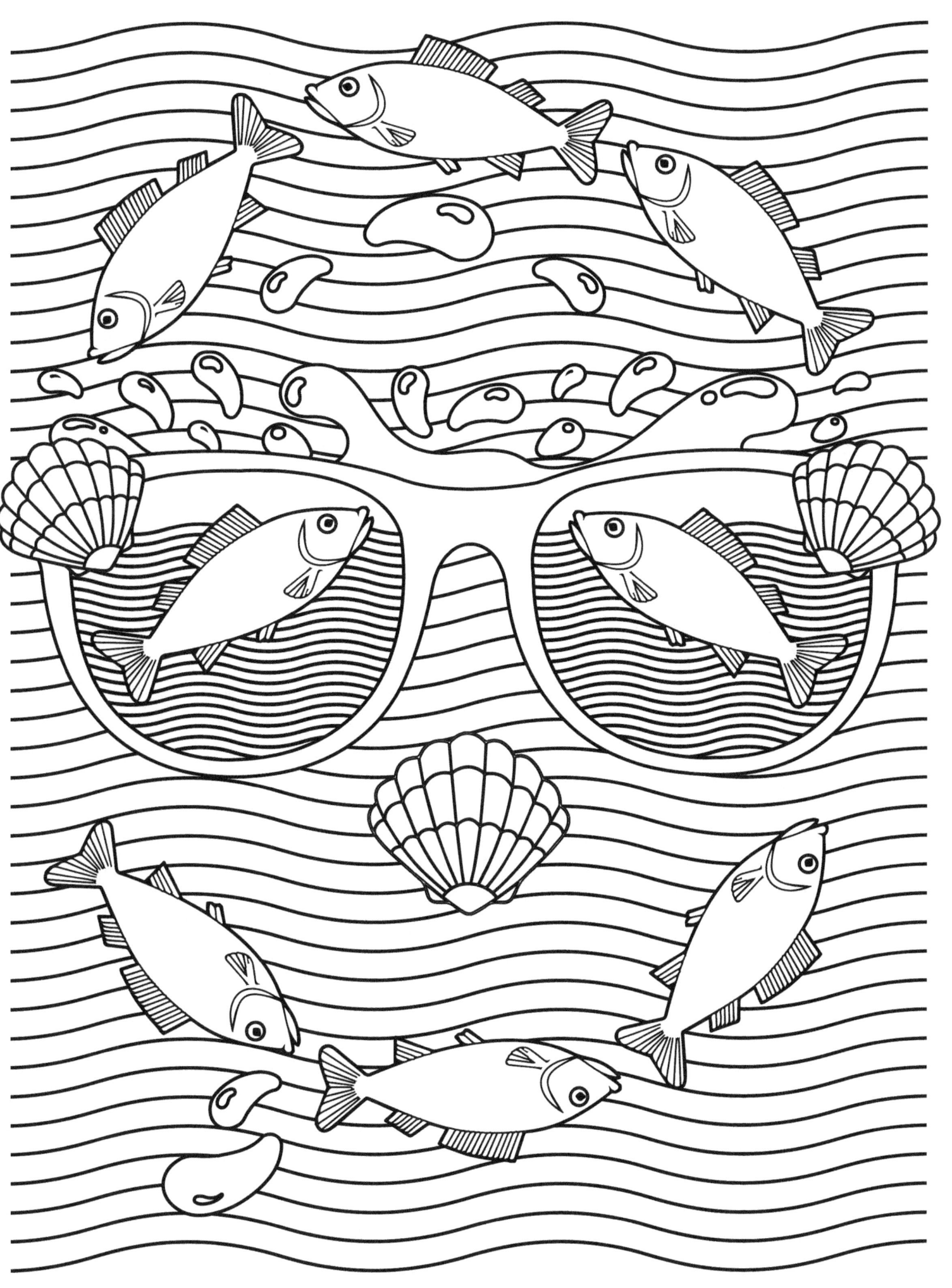

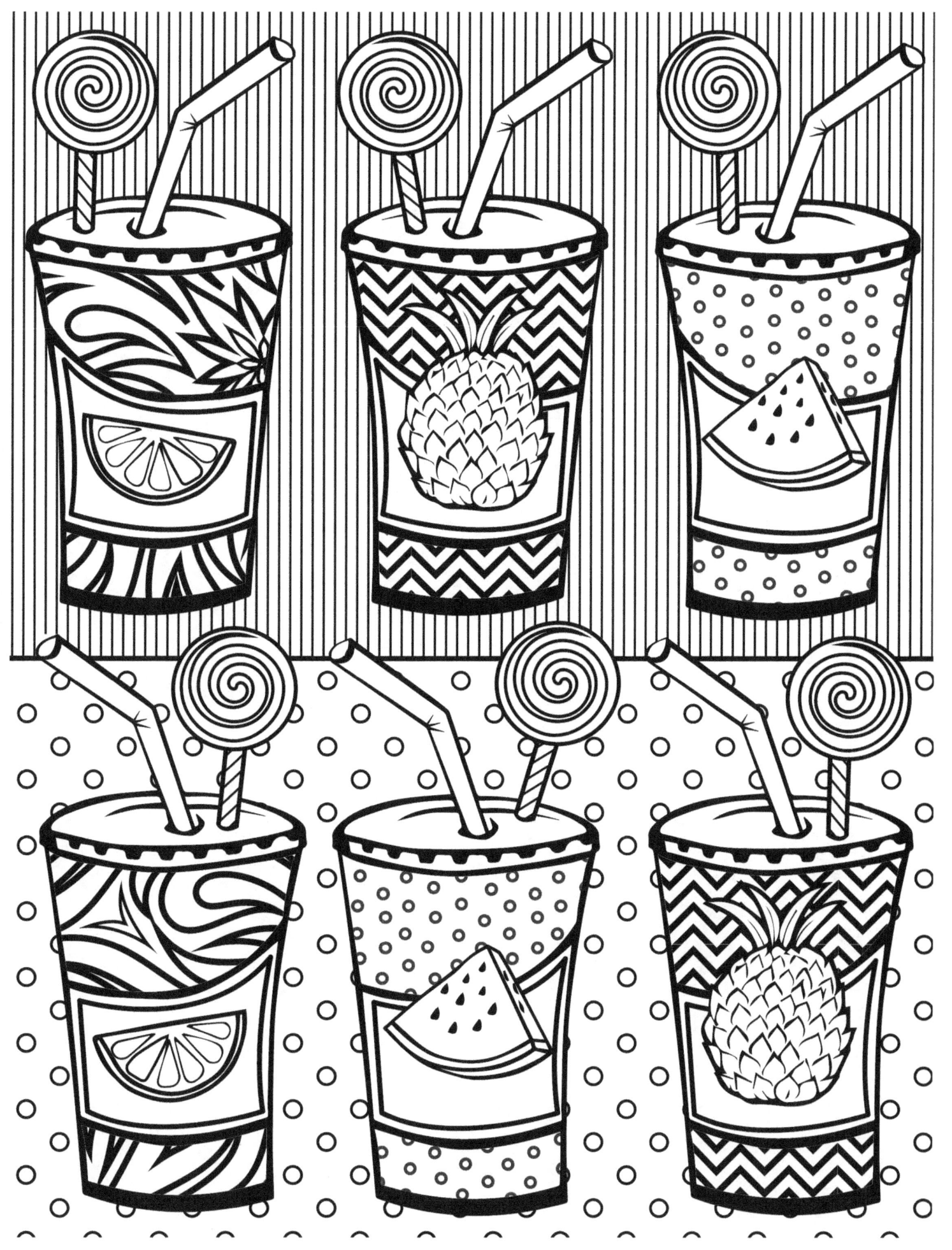

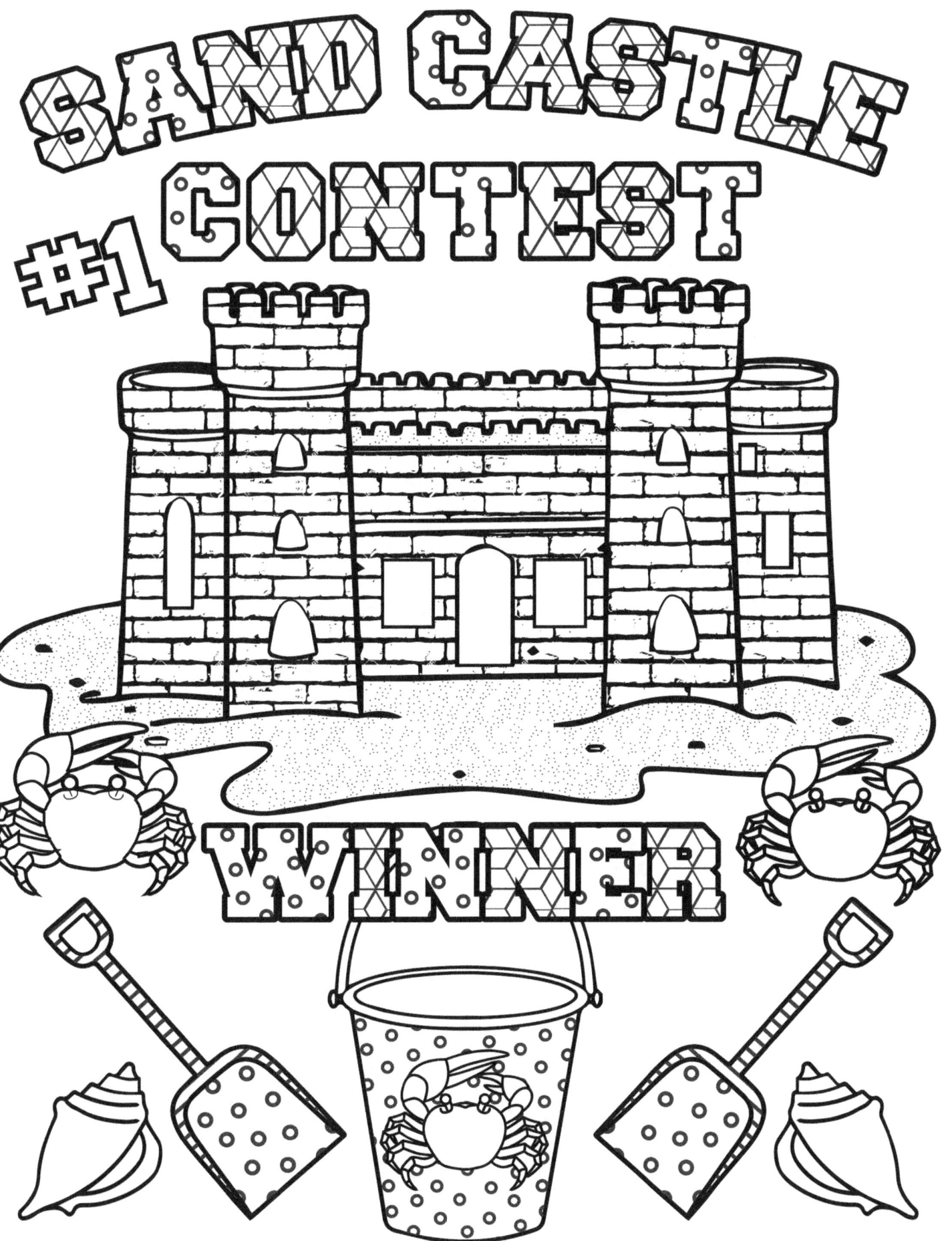

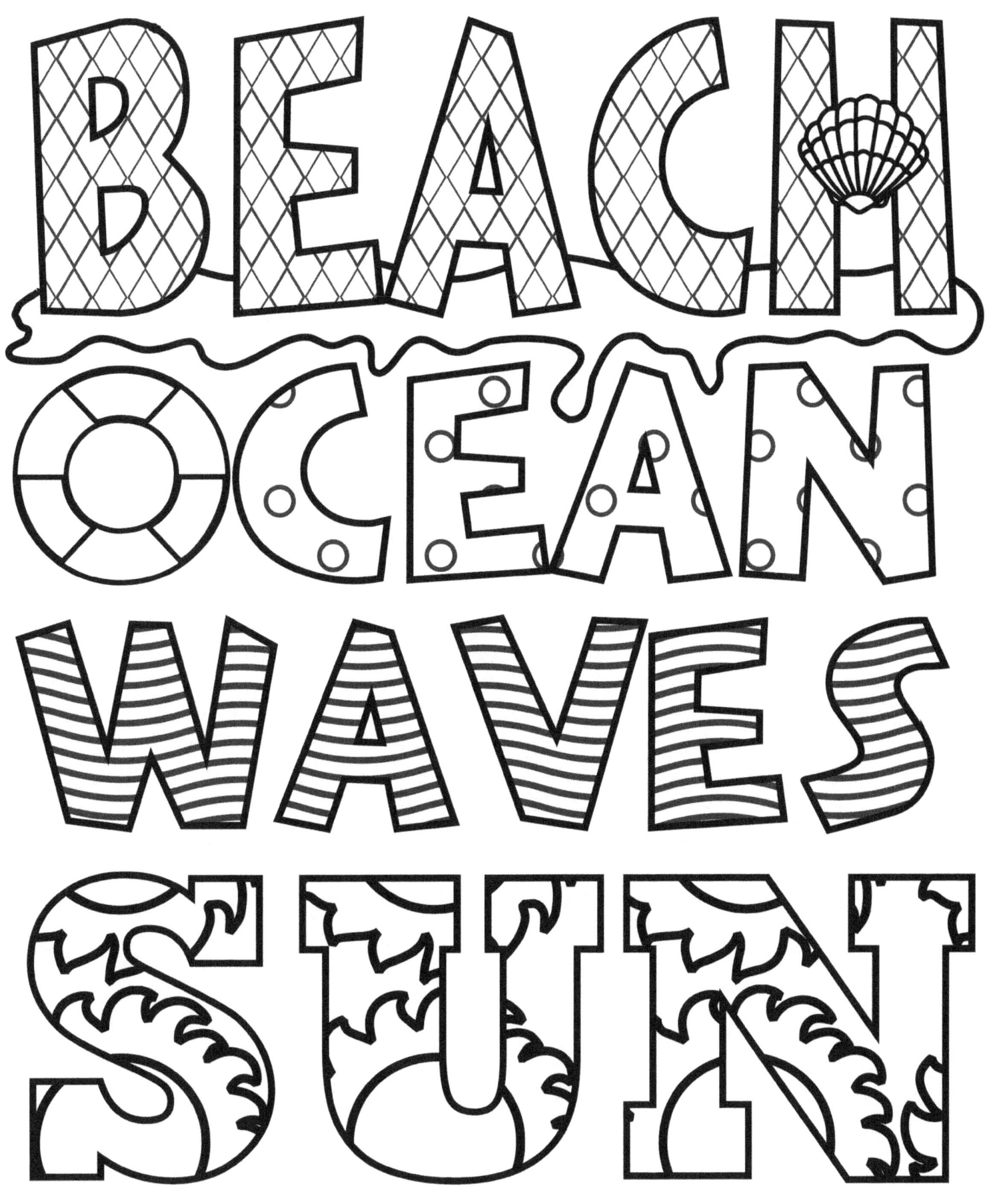

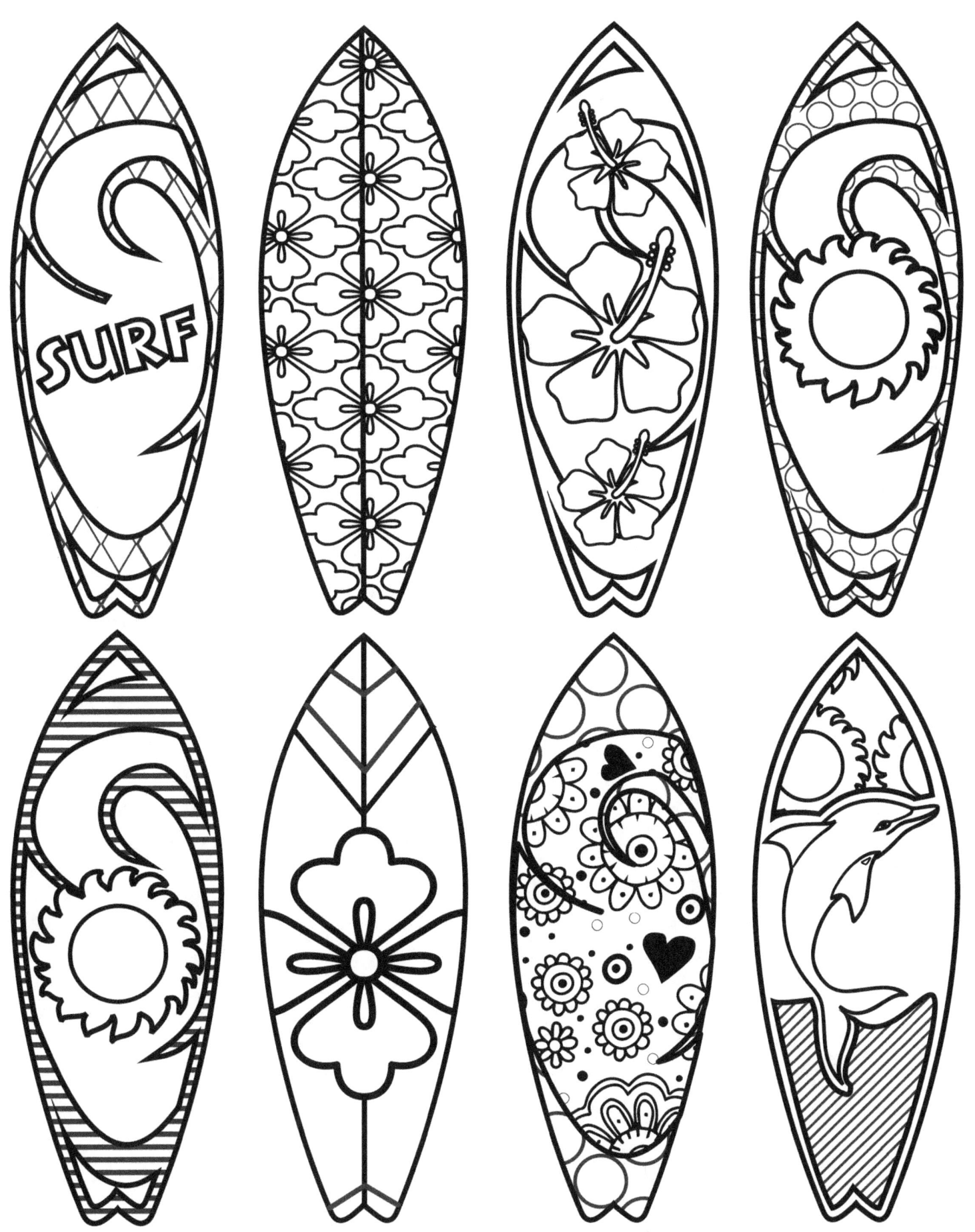

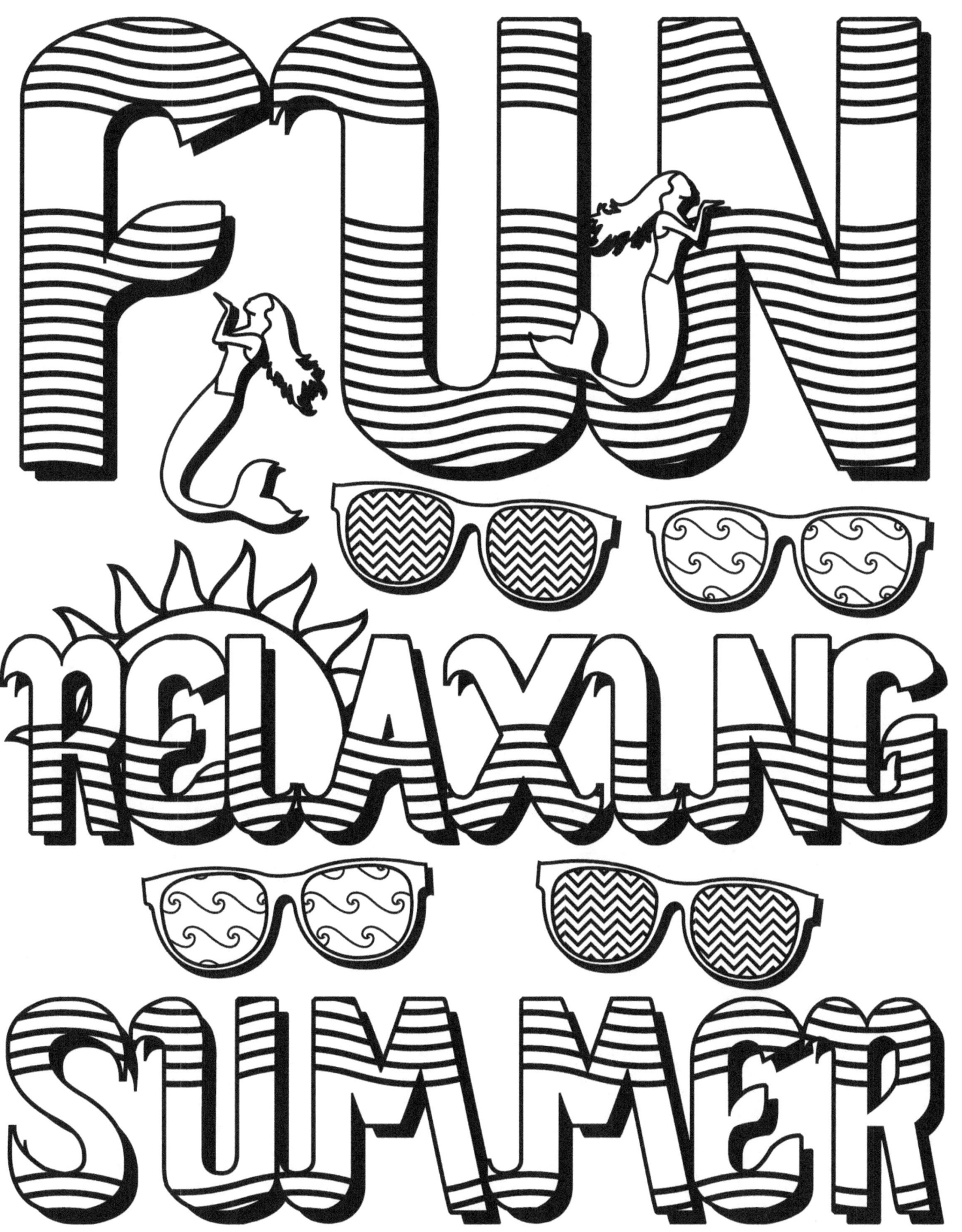

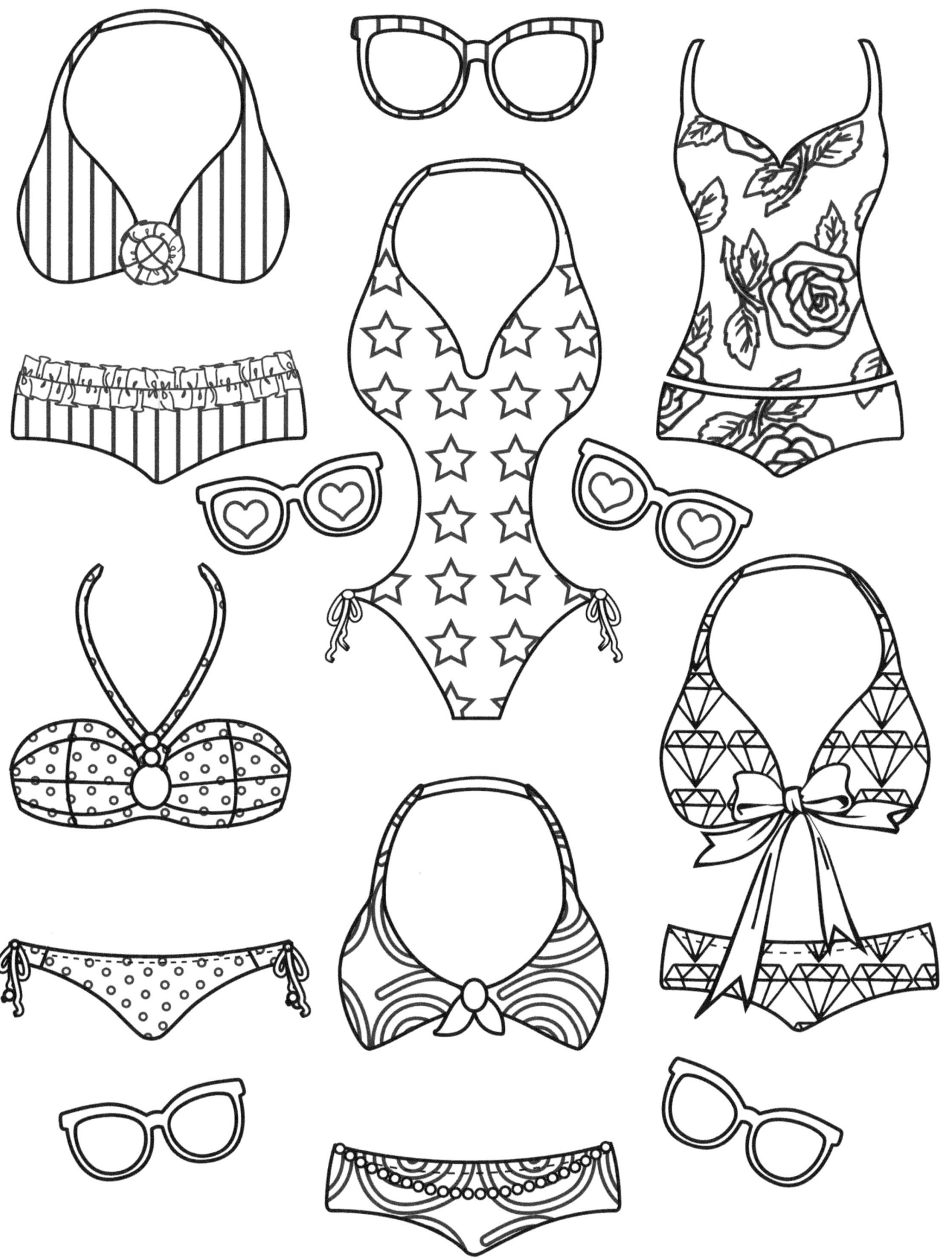

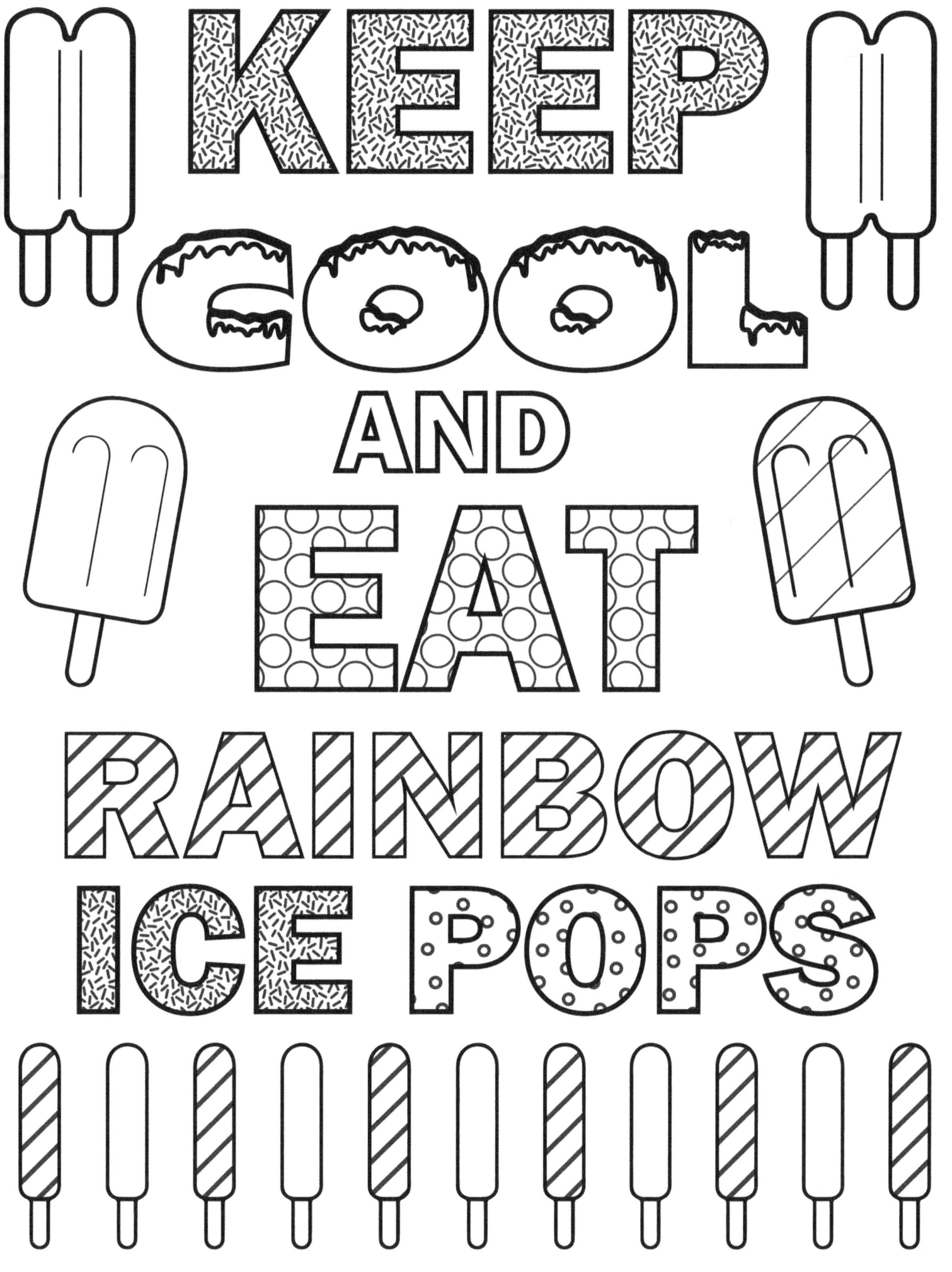